A+ books

POLAR ANIMALS

ARCTIC FOXES
ARE AWESOME

by Jaclyn Jaycox

Consultant: Greg Breed
Associate Professor of Ecology
Institute of Arctic Biology
University of Alaska, Fairbanks

PEBBLE
a capstone imprint

A+ Books are published by Pebble,
1710 Roe Crest Drive, North Mankato, Minnesota 56003
www.mycapstone.com

Library of Congress Cataloging-in-Publication Data
Names: Jaycox, Jaclyn, 1983–author.
Title: Arctic Foxes Are Awesome / by Jaclyn Jaycox.
Description: North Mankato, Minnesota : an imprint of Pebble, [2020]
   | Series: A+. Polar Animals | Audience: Age 4–8. | Audience: K to Grade 3.
   | Includes bibliographical references and index.
Identifiers: LCCN 2018055879| ISBN 9781977108142 (hardcover) | ISBN
   9781977109941 (paperback) | ISBN 9781977108234 (ebook pdf)
Subjects: LCSH: Arctic fox—Juvenile literature.
Classification: LCC QL737.C22 J38 2020 | DDC 599.776/4—dc23
LC record available at https://lccn.loc.gov/2018055879

Editorial Credits
Nikki Potts, editor; Kayla Rossow, designer; Morgan Walters, media researcher;
Laura Manthe, production specialist

Photo Credits
Alamy: All Canada Photos, 5, National Geographic Image Collection, 13; Getty Images: DAN GURAVICH, 25, John E Marriott, 22, Steven Kazlowski, 17; Newscom: Sergey Gorshkov, 14, Sergey Gorshkov, 18; Shutterstock: Andrew Astbury, 16, critterbiz, bottom right 24, Erni, 9, Gail Johnson, 11, Giedriius, 19, Glass and Nature, 20, 29, Jamen Percy, 10, Jean-Edouard Rozey, 27, Josef Pittner, 21, Jukka Jantunen, 23, jWolskyPhotography, 8, Mara008, design element (blue), Neil Burton, spread 6-7, nialat, 28, Oliay, design element (ice window), outdoorsman, Cover, photosoft, design element (ice), Pixeljoy, 26, Through Christy's Lens, 15, Tony Campbell, 4, Vlada Cech, bottom left 24

All internet sites appearing in back matter were available and accurate when this book was sent to press.

Note to Parents, Teachers, and Librarians

This Polar Animals book uses full-color photographs and a nonfiction format to introduce the concept of Arctic foxes. *Arctic Foxes Are Awesome* is designed to be read aloud to a pre-reader or to be read independently by an early reader. Photographs help listeners and early readers understand the text and concepts discussed. The book encourages further learning by including the following sections: Table of Contents, Glossary, Read More, Internet Sites, Critical Thinking Questions, and Index. Early readers may need assistance using these features.

TABLE OF CONTENTS

The Great Hunter

Shhh. The Arctic fox listens. It hears something beneath the snow.

Suddenly, the fox springs into the air. It lands and breaks through the snow. The fox has caught its prey!

Furry Foxes

Arctic foxes have small ears. But they have great hearing. Their legs and noses are short.

Arctic foxes can weigh up to 20 pounds (9 kilograms). They are about 2 feet (0.6 meters) long.

Arctic foxes have thick, white coats. They have big, fluffy tails. Their coats and tails keep them warm. Foxes wrap their long tails around them like blankets.

Large tails also help foxes to stay balanced as they walk on snow and ice.

Arctic foxes live in the Arctic tundra. It is one of the coldest places on Earth. The Arctic has long winters and short summers. White fur helps foxes blend into the snow. They hide from predators.

During summer, foxes'
fur turns brown or gray.
Then they blend in with
rocks and plants.

Arctic foxes live in burrows. They dig their homes into hills or rocks. Burrows have tunnels. Some burrows are as big as a football field! Burrows can have many entrances. In a blizzard, Arctic foxes may dig into the snow for shelter.

Finding Food

Arctic foxes move from place to place to find food. They eat small mammals, such as lemmings. Arctic foxes can eat up to 12 lemmings a day!

Foxes also eat birds, fish, and bugs. They eat plants and berries too. Arctic foxes drink water from streams. They also eat snow.

Arctic foxes have a strong sense of smell. It helps them find food under the snow and ice.

Foxes sometimes follow bigger animals. They eat what the larger animals leave behind. During summer, Arctic foxes store food in their burrows. They save the food for winter.

Family Life

Female foxes give birth to pups in the spring. Arctic fox pups are called kits.

Most litters have between five and nine kits. Some have as many as 14 kits! Kits stay in the burrow with their mother. She feeds them milk and keeps them warm. The father guards the den.

A group of Arctic foxes is called a skulk. A mother, father, and kits make up a skulk. Sometimes there is another female. She helps take care of the kits.

The skulk splits up when
the kits are 6 months old.
Arctic foxes live alone until
the next mating season.

Ruff, ruff!

Arctic foxes bark at each other. They usually only do this during mating season.

Arctic foxes also yip and
howl. These sounds warn
kits that danger is near.

Staying Safe

Arctic foxes live about three to six years in the wild. They have many predators. Polar bears and wolves hunt them. Wolves and snowy owls eat kits. People trap foxes for their fur.

Wolf

Snowy Owl

The changing climate is a threat to Arctic foxes. Temperatures in the Arctic are rising. Ice melts. Water rises. Less ice changes the foxes' habitat. They may have less to eat. It may be harder for them to survive.

Arctic foxes live in cold places. Their thick fur keeps them warm. Their hearing and sense of smell make them great hunters.

These awesome polar animals are small. But they are tough!

GLOSSARY

Arctic (ARK-tik)—the area near the North Pole; the Arctic is cold and covered with ice

blizzard (BLIZ-erd)—a heavy snowstorm with strong wind; a blizzard can last several days

burrow (BUHR-oh)—a hole or tunnel in the ground used as a house

den (DEN)—a place where a wild animal may live; a den may be a hole in the ground or a trunk of a tree

female (FEE-male)—a mammal that can give birth to young animals or lay eggs

habitat (HAB-uh-tat)—the natural place and conditions in which a plant or animal lives

howl (HOUL)—to make a loud, sad-sounding noise

litter (LIT-ur)—a group of animals born at the same time to the same mother

mammal (MAM-uhl)—a warm-blooded animal that breathes air; female mammals feed milk to their young

mate (MATE)—to join together to produce young

polar (POH-lar)—having to do with the icy regions around the North or South Pole

predator (PRED-uh-tur)—an animal that hunts other animals for food

prey (PRAY)—an animal hunted by another animal for food

shelter (SHEL-tur)—a safe, covered place

threat (THRET)—something that can be considered dangerous

trap (TRAP)—to catch animals using a device that springs shut suddenly

tundra (TUHN-druh)—a cold area where trees do not grow; the soil under the ground in the tundra is permanently frozen

READ MORE

Gardeski, Christina Mia. *All About the North and South Poles.*
Habitats. North Mankato, MN: Capstone Press, 2017.

Person, Stephen. *Arctic Fox: Very Cool!* Uncommon Animals.
New York: Bearport Publishing, 2017.

Statts, Leo. *Arctic Foxes.* Zoom in on Polar Animals.
Minneapolis: Abdo Zoom, 2017.

INTERNET SITES

Arctic Kingdom, Top 10 Fun Facts About Arctic Foxes
https://arctickingdom.com/10-fun-facts-about-arctic-fox/

Active Wild, Arctic Fox Facts
https://www.activewild.com/arctic-fox-facts/

CRITICAL THINKING QUESTIONS

1. What do Arctic foxes use their tails for?

2. The warming climate is causing Arctic foxes' habitat to change. What is a habitat? (Hint: Use the glossary for help!)

3. What do Arctic foxes eat?

INDEX